"DON'T TELL ME I CAN'T"

Living life to its fullest as told by a woman who's doing just that.

SUSAN M. STRAND

Pageant winner, Pan Am purser,
Helicopter pilot, Park ranger,
Naturalist, Motivational speaker

ISBN: 978-1-7923-9916-9

Library of Congress: NRC109838

Inquires may be made to Hoverbug@gmail.com

Cover design by Far Lands Publishing
Interior design by Heidi Hansen
Edited by Linda B. Myers

DEDICATION

To the Lord and my parents.

TABLE OF CONTENTS

A NOTE FROM THE EDITORS

Susan M. Strand was born in the decade following WWII. Women worked during the war in occupations traditionally held by men, and many never returned to the farm or the housewife role. They taught their daughters to want more options for themselves. These were early days in the massive move to destroy glass ceilings.

Susan believed she could attempt nearly anything. Her parents imparted the idea that trying was the most important part of success. She rose from roots of poverty and a learning disability – plus a harrowing three months in a vegetative coma – to live the life she chose, unfettered by naysayers.

She defeated sexism by working her way around it through superior performance when possible. And when not able to avoid it, she fought it head on. Susan played pivotal roles as a purser in the early days of Pan Am on flights in and out of Vietnam to provide our soldiers with days of R and R. Later, she served the planes carrying the Presidential press core. She visited most of the globe when women rarely traveled alone. Purely for the right to become a helicopter pilot, she joined the army when she was twice the age of the other recruits. In her early retirement years, she was a naturalist on cruise ships after years of surviving the bureaucracy of the National Park system.

Susan remains a quiet, reserved woman in command of her own well-being. When it was suggested she write her story, her first reaction was, "Who'd want to read about me?"

The answer? Anyone battling their way through life. Anyone who must conquer the obstacles they face. Anyone with dreams and aspirations. In telling her story, Susan M. Strand gives the people who listen a very valuable blueprint for living the life they choose for themselves.

PREFACE

Even if you were born with a silver spoon in your mouth, success is not guaranteed. After all, you might choke on it. To succeed is hard work. Like any fascinating game or story, it has obstacles to overcome and pains to endure and bad guys to defeat.

It's easy to blame something else for not fulfilling your wish. Maybe you have screwed up parents, maybe poverty or addiction plagues you, maybe a learning disability gets in your way, maybe wars and pandemics interfere. If you look for reasons to fail, you'll find them. But the opposite is also true: if you look for reasons to succeed, you'll find them. I choose to concentrate on this end of the spectrum.

So how do you succeed? Well first, let's define success. To me, it means doing your best to overcome what you can and outfox what you can't. To overcome or to outfox both require *perseverance*. That is the basis for living the life you want. It is a tool you must have regardless of race, gender, or age.

This is a book about success through perseverance. Get comfortable with that word because I'm hoping you'll use it a lot on your own journey. If you keep at it, if you take aim right at your goal without wavering, you'll very likely reach it. You must never quit. Learn to zigzag around impediments. To knock aside bullies and critics and naysayers. That's how you keep on the path that you alone choose.

I did. It wasn't fast or easy. This isn't my life story, but it is a tale about the times perseverance got me through the gullies in life and back to the peaks. How perseverance helped me climb out of financial need and disability to take flight as one of the first female helicopter pilots.

You'll find my thoughts on other weapons of success, as well … weapons like self-esteem, self-reliance, and fear management. You must be proud of who you are; there is nobody else like you, with your unique gift to offer the rest of us. I hope you find something here that helps you on your way. You should never have to look back and say I wish I had; live to say I'm glad I did.

I found inspiration in Robert Frost's poem and took the road less travelled

PART 1
REACH FOR THE STARS

CHAPTER ONE

The Flying Bicycle

When I was five, I was given an old Schwinn that my dad found in an alley. Fixed up with white walls, streamers, shiny red and white tubes … wow! To me, it was the bomb. The trouble was, it was full sized, and I was pint sized.

"Why didn't you get her a trike, Lloyd? Something her own size!" Neighbors up and down the street would yell to my dad.

"She'll grow into it," he yelled back. Nobody accused my dad of ever wasting a nickel.

I couldn't sit on the seat of the 26-inch bike because I couldn't reach it. I had to stand to pedal, my little hands clutched at eye level around the handlebars. It was insane. I fell and got up, fell and got up. My elbows and knees had scabs for months.

And then they didn't. I road to the end of the block and back. Around the block. To the park. And on into life. I called her Betsy, after Davy Crockett's rifle in the TV series. I could fly on that bike while the other kids chugged along on training wheels.

Was I a success because it was the only bike I was going to get? Maybe. I think it's my first memory of my own perseverance. People said I couldn't do it. And they were proved wrong.

Without a doubt, a child will find a personality trait to exploit if her parents nurture it. My mom had gone from immigrant farm girl to a Rosie the Riveter; nobody knew more about persistence than she did. My father instilled in me the belief that you're never a failure as long as you try your best. Not a bad set of values to start you on your way, right?

But it still wasn't easy.

Bullies. Ugh!

I was bullied in school, although back then, it was rarely as vicious as it is for many young people today. Still, I was teased for failing kindergarten (it was an administrative error, but the other kids didn't concern themselves with the truth). One boy pushed me onto the cement at recess and broke my tooth. A silver cap gleamed from my new front tooth for months after that. I was a laughingstock at the ripe old age of five.

Another youngster shot our mailbox with BBs to attract my attention. A pellet went through our window and nearly hit me. I was horrified, not to mention my parents' reactions.

Riding the bus bordered on gangland warfare among grade-schoolers. The name-calling was hurtful as bee stings. I learned to hide my fear because the less reaction from me, the less interesting I became to abusers. Learning to handle fear would come in handy years later against alligators, bears, bullets, and flight surgeons.

The Upside of "Eavesdropping"

Money was an issue growing up (hence, the used bike). Dad worked in real estate, and Mom worked with him part-time. But when I was home—after school or in the summers—she was there. She watched over me with the ferocity of a she-bear, ensuring that I learned good sportsmanship along with playground games. She pulled stickers out of my feet from running barefoot during track at school under the hot Phoenix sun.

One evening, I overheard a conversation in the kitchen. Mom told my dad there was only one hundred dollars in their checking account. She felt she needed to get a job. I was seven when I learned that scary adult reality: nothing fills your pantry for free. My parents were in such a financial bind that, like it or not, Mom must work full time.

She said to Dad, "I think Susan could handle being at home alone."

I was baffled. *Me!* I was a burden that kept Mom from working. I hated the thought. From that day forward, I did everything I could to prove I could survive on my own. I'd be dependable, by golly. It was a quick way to grow up, shouldering the responsibilities of keeping out of trouble. I learned to make breakfast that wasn't burnt, bake, clean the house, do laundry, and even iron a white dress shirt.

Did I miss being the center of my mother's universe? Well, sure. But I was sort of tickled, too. My parents trusted me. Their ability to rely on me was a great boost to my self-esteem. I was proud of myself. When you have the self-reliance to deliver on another person's trust in you, you can take on almost any situation you are in.

"I Wish I Had"

As an "eavesdropping" child, I heard another snippet of conversation that was to change my life. At a party, I overheard a man tell Dad, "I wish I'd done that with my life." Now there was a puzzle. This big guy was free to do what he chose in an adult world, or so it seemed to me. Why on earth wouldn't he? What had stopped him?

How sad that seemed in the eyes of a child. With the self-esteem of one who conquered a too-big bike, I vowed that would never happen to me. I didn't yet know things could conspire against you. I didn't even know what I wanted to be, but I was sure I'd get there.

I'd never have to say, "I wish I had."

The Biggest Hurdle

I was a reserved child, shy and unsure. It wasn't always easy to develop belief in myself, especially since I had to overcome an obstacle that accompanied me through grade school, high school, and beyond. I had what today would be called a learning disability. I could not read and retain easily. If I let up, my grades slipped. To stay even in the middle of the class, I had to read, read, and read again to pass tests.

Was it fair? Heavens, no. Did I give up? Come on now, what have I been saying about perseverance? All it meant was I had to work harder than many of the other kids to pass tests. Some of them were living through nightmares far worse than my own. Comparing backgrounds is useless unless looking for reasons to justify failure. And I've always hated that word.

Playing the Game

As a child, I wasn't allowed to take shop or play football. "That isn't for girls," my school authorities said. I was too young in those days to call foul on that nonsense. But I learned to ice skate, ride horses, and fly on a bicycle. I joined the basketball team, and I played with a football at recess anyway. I was no shrinking violet.

Although I joined nearly every team, from track to soccer; as I grew up, I didn't excel at any one in particular. However, I was athletic enough to be a go-to kid in all of them. I helped others where I could. I was never taught that you must be the best; I was taught the important thing was to try. And in the trying, I surprised myself by how much more I could achieve than anyone had thought possible. By trying to be the best I could be, I was even better.

At the end of our eighth-grade honors assembly, awards were handed out to the accomplished athletes. Then one was given that had never been given before. My coach presented me with the school's first award for Good Sportsmanship.

To this day, of all the honors I have won, it is my favorite.

SIDE-NOTE: Good sportsmanship

You better believe that good sportsmanship is important for more than personal popularity. Getting along with your team is a microcosm of the world at large; it's a great place to learn how to manage in society and come out ahead of the game.

Skills like the art of compromise and negotiation and strategy are essential on the sports field. You can use those tools elsewhere throughout your life. "My way or the highway" is a belief system that almost guarantees a failure in a civilized world. You'll find your path easier if others want to hike it with you. And maybe, just maybe, another player does have a better idea; you might learn something from them of great value to you.

CHAPTER TWO

Do What Needs Done

I had to give up some things in order to study. In high school, I played sports, but I didn't go out for cheerleading. I didn't hang in malt shops with the gang. I didn't date very much. It's not that it wouldn't have been fun. It's not that my parents didn't allow it. It's that it wasn't the best use of my time if I wanted my life to unfold in a direction that would satisfy me in the long run. I had to study for long hours.

I knew I had to build up my self-esteem as well. So, I took on two tasks that made me shake like a leaf but forced me out of my shell. First, I ran for Student's Executive Committee, and second, I entered the Junior Miss Pageant. I didn't win, but the experience was life-changing for me. I learned forever more that trying matters more than winning when it comes to success. I didn't win a crown, but I became more confident, formed lasting friendships, had fun, and discovered I could be quite the ham, and I call all that a great success!

It's a choice only you can make to live for today or for what the future holds. It's one of the tolls that perseverance demands of you. All I can say is that today is very short while the future should last a very long time. You do the math.

If You Can't Scale a Wall, Go Around It

I studied hard in high school to earn a college scholarship in order to help out financially. But since both parents worked, I was denied the opportunity even though I was in the upper ten percent of my class. Well, duh! Why were they both working if not for the financial need?

I remember being plenty upset by this surprising situation. But I didn't change my goal … I just changed my destination. Arizona State University wasn't my first choice, but it was the college my folks could afford. I wanted to work to help out, but they knew how difficult it was for me to pass my courses. They said they'd make it work. And they did.

SIDE-NOTE: The Good Luck of Love

Having a supportive family makes everything easier. I was blessed with wonderful parents and family. My favorite summers were on my grandparents' farm, running wild with my cousins, building forts, and inventing games. My grandmother gave us her all, well, maybe except the recipe for her chocolate chip cookies. I tried to drag it out of her. It went like this:

"Grandma, how much flour are you putting in the bowl?"

"Oh, I don't know. Maybe a couple of cups."

"Well, how much sugar?"

"Maybe a couple handfuls."

"Vanilla?"

"Maybe one of these spoonsful." She held up an ancient utensil worn from work.

I tried, but her chocolate chip cookie recipe followed her to the grave.

How joyful it is to have loving memories like this, having family in your corner. My cousins and I are close to this day. I can't imagine how much harder it is when you don't have these bonds. But it is possible to overcome almost any obstacle. You can do it. I believe in you. More on this in a little while.

CHAPTER THREE

College Days

I majored in International Affairs. I wanted to learn all about the world and see its every corner. I'd met Barry Goldwater in high school, and he had inspired me to discover more about foreign service if I was truly interested in international events.

But I knew college would be hard for me, a smalltown kid who had to keep her nose to the grindstone just to survive. So the very first thing I did was pledge a sorority. Oh, not to party. I knew I'd need the support of people close to me. I figured life within a sorority meant more assistance than a dorm alone could offer. If I had to study more than others, well, "sisters" would accept that I did. They'd help make sure I was left alone to stay on task. And they did, bless them.

But only after two events that rattled my little world.

My sorority sisters wanted me to go to a frat party with them. "C'mon, Susan. It'll be fun. Boys! Or, er, college men!"

Sure, I thought. But then I lectured myself. *You won't know what you truly want if you don't try new things, Susan.* Finally, I compromised. "Okay, if I go and don't like it, will you give it a rest after that? Let me study in peace?"

"Absolutely! But you'll love it. Promise."

I hated every second. The packed crowd of strangers too close … inappropriate groping … yelling to be heard … thick smoke … fumes of booze … acid rock so loud it made my head vibrate. What was fun for some was a nightmare for me.

My sorority sisters lived up to their part of the bargain after that traumatic experience. I was different, yes, but I was still one of them, so they gave me the space I needed to pass my courses. But they got me once again, although this time, the results were far better. They signed me up for the Miss Wool of Arizona pageant. And I won!

Miss Wool

Chances are pretty good that you've never heard of Miss Wool, but in rural states, it was a big deal. It meant I could travel, go to cities where

I'd never been, and represent the wool growers of Arizona. I had to overcome my fear of public speaking and my fear of being the center of attention. I met state governors and celebrities.

The only truly embarrassing part was having Donald O'Conner sing *"Look at that face"* to me on national TV. I had no idea what to do with that face as he crooned!

The pageant year widened my horizons about people a long way from Phoenix. It deepened my interest in international relations, and the Miss Wool contest gave me a firm platform to crack that anxious shell of mine further open. Fear lost its power to hold me back from trying new things. I recommend you try something that you find intimidating (short of standing in front of a logging truck or crossing a high wire between buildings). Volunteer to teach kids to read, try another trick on your skateboard, recite a poem to your class, or supervise a neighborhood victory garden. *What* you do doesn't matter as much as *that* you do. You'll find fear can turn into a whole lot of fun.

I owe those sneaky sorority women a lot. Wherever they are today, I thank them for helping me avoid "I wish I had."

When Bad Things Happen

I'm not naïve; I know unexpected events can stop you in your tracks. I'll tell you about mine in just a second. But first, remember this: you can't stop misfortune, but you may be able to control how you handle it.

Let's say your best friend dies. Or you are diagnosed with a disease. Or a trusted boyfriend dumps you. You will feel that life is over.

But be patient. Don't act out in anger or grief, or pain in any way that won't allow you a second chance. No drugs, no violence, and for heaven's sake, no suicide. You WILL recover from the bad news, the loss, the hurt. Recovery is a journey, and no one—not a doctor, a friend, a parent— can tell you how long it will take. Just keep at it, and you will arrive on the other side. There's always hope, and miraculous things can happen.

My Calamity

It was my junior year. My life was going along perfectly. I was young, loved school, had new friends, and knew big things were ahead. On a Sunday evening, when my parents were driving me back to the dorm, everything changed. It's the last thing I remember for many weeks to come. There was no way of knowing I was steps away from death's door.

Instead of going to school, my frantic parents took me to an emergency room where they had no idea what to do with me. In case it was a nervous breakdown—which my parents knew wasn't the situation—a doctor gave me a shot to calm me down.

I'd never had any of the symptoms like fever, seizure, sensitivity to light, or headaches. I merely stopped daily life and sank into a deep coma. No amount of medical knowledge available at that time could explain this mysterious encephalitis that crept over me. I was such a mystery to them; I broke the local record for the number of EEGs given to one person.

I could not be reached, even by the love of my desperate parents. Weeks passed. I registered no brain waves. I was not on life support; I was breathing on my own. But that was the only sign of life, and that's how the future looked for me.

After three months, decision time came. I was braindead, according to the surgeons. My parents were told if I ever came out of the coma, I would be in a vegetative state. If the surgeons were allowed to operate on my brain, I would die, but knowledge might be gained to help others. Imagine parents faced with that choice for their only child.

On the morning of the surgery, one of the doctors said he'd dreamed he was supposed to speak to me in German. He didn't really know the language but gave a few words a try. I opened my eyes and answered in German.

Another EEG was ordered, and I was fine.

What had happened? I'd been studying German in school. Maybe that unexpected language so close to me caused my brain to grab hold of a word or two. I don't know. But I believe someone watches over you to help you through your darkest moments. And like they say, miracles happen every day.

Recovery

I remember none of those three months in a coma. As far as I was concerned, those weeks never happened at all. And that length of time cut out of my awareness became its own problem.

I was shattered, mentally and physically when I came to. I had caused my parents such pain. I often became confused about time and events. My mother would calmly explain what happened to me when I felt lost. Everything had gone on without me. My college classes, my sorority, my plans.

After that amount of time lying comatose in a bed, I was weakened bodily as well as mentally. I'd lost so much muscle. I kept thinking I was fine, but I found I could no longer lift a loaded book bag. I couldn't even ride Betsy, my beloved bike.

Yet I was determined to pick up where I left off, to finish out my college years with the rest of my class. Achieving that goal became my beacon as clear as a lighthouse. I was still weak when I signed up for summer school in order to catch up. My doctors and therapists poo-pooed my ability to do this. It was as hard for them to understand that the coma meant nothing to me as it was for me to understand it meant everything to them. They couldn't grasp that I didn't consider myself sick ... those months never happened as far as I was concerned.

They didn't count on my lifelong companions: the Lord and perseverance. With the help and understanding of a whole lot of people, I built myself back up and graduated on time. Life in the big wide world of employment was about to begin.

PART II
THE MOST EXPERIENCED AIRLINE

Susan Strand in her Pan Am designer uniform

CHAPTER ONE

Earning My Wings

In my senior year, a college friend became a recruiter for Pan American World Airways. She let me know they were interviewing for stewardesses.

Stewardess? Me? It had never crossed my mind. If I'd thought about it, I probably would have preferred the cockpit to the cabins! But women weren't pilots yet, not with the big carriers.

I went to the interview in Phoenix because you explore whatever opportunity comes your way; they often arrive in disguise. Do a little digging, be open to new concepts, and take a few risks if you hope to grow.

Literally, hundreds of women showed up for that interview. The line snaked outside the building. Good grief! But I persisted, and I learned a thing or two I hadn't realized before:

Getting such a job was insanely difficult. I heard it said that a higher percentage of applicants to Harvard were accepted than applicants to flight attendant jobs at Pan Am. You needed a college degree and the knowledge of at least one foreign language to qualify. You must have demonstrable communication skills, poise in the face of potential emergencies, and a track record of studying hard until your lessons are second nature.

From the large flock of smart, talented, sparkling women wanting to be chosen to fly, I was one of only four selected that day. Was I lucky? Sure. Lady Luck always plays a part. She can bring a chance your way … but it's almost always up to your own preparation and perseverance to close the deal.

Consider the Context

I went from questioning the job to wanting it, all in a day of interviews! If you are surprised, think steppingstone. When you are about to cross an alligator-infested swamp (an apt description of the job market), always look for steppingstones. You won't get to the other bank without them. Becoming a stewardess on an international carrier could well be my opening to a career in international service.

Consider what it was like so many decades ago; in those years, flight attendants were respected. I didn't have to deal with the air rage or hazmat-like conditions faced today. Stewards and stewardesses had careers that were seen as glamorous as long ago as the 1930s. By now, of course, things have changed. Flying as a passenger is no longer an occasion to dress up; it's not considered an elitist activity. For a while, those serving aboard became a laughingstock to some or a fantasy sex goddess to others. Several air carriers lowered their standards to hot pants uniforms or to ad campaigns like, "Hi, I'm Cheryl. Fly me."

But this was 1969. Many airlines, especially the international carriers, treated their attendants in a dignified manner. Pan Am remained focused on safety and service, not on "trolley dollies" or "coffee, tea or me." They turned away from many mortifying agist and sexist qualifications. They offered us stylish uniforms (mine designed by Edith Head and Evan Picone to name just two) that were modest and serviceable on a flight. Best of all, they flew across the oceans. It all seemed like quite an opportunity for an International Affairs graduate with a minor in languages.

In addition to wanting the job to expand my horizons, I was delighted to follow my mother into the aviation world. During WWII, she worked in the Midwest for the Civilian Signal Corp repairing radios for aircraft and tanks. When she landed a job in Seattle at Boeing, she moved to "the wild west," away from her North Dakota family, doing what she could for the war effort. As I mentioned earlier, she was a genuine Rosie the Riveter. Mom worked on Boeing bombers … and now I was about to work on Boeing jets. My family history has a long line of aviation specialists, be they pilots, gate agents, flight attendants, or reservationists. Threads like this are the connections that hold families together.

Two-Month Stewardess Training

My training began in Miami in June, a month after graduating from Arizona State in 1969. We learned about Pan Am, from its beginnings in the 1920s through its current use of the slogan, "the most experienced airline." Emergency procedures were at the top of the list of skills to master. Individual passenger needs were next, whether it was the right wine or the way to conquer a fear of flying. We all buffed up our knowledge of foreign languages in the lab provided for us during the two months we trained (there was a language lab at every Pan Am base as well). We believed that the Pan Am attendant knew her way around the world like most people know their way around the block.

SIDE-NOTE: A Life Lesson Learned

After graduating from training school, you could request a base location to begin your career. Five of us were selected for Los Angeles. Four of the women chose to rent an apartment together, leaving me out in the cold. Were my feelings hurt? Of course! Like a slap in the face

One of the girls disliked me for being what she called "too perfect." So here was a novel life lesson: people could be mean-spirited.

My parents, teachers, and friends always seemed pleased when I excelled. I was dumbfounded by the kind of jealousy or disapproval or general snarky-ness that makes you question who you are.

I've learned since that there are always critics, people eager to stand in your way. Today I say ignore them if you can; don't let them divert you. Given time, they may come around. Or not. The problem is their craziness to solve, not yours.

Still, I sympathize if you find it happening to you. Some cohorts, co-workers, and alleged friends are not the allies they seem. Just stay your course. It is pivotal to a successful life of pride in what you do. You'll find that many acquaintances will come around to your way of thinking, and that your true supporters will help you along the way. Those who don't? Well, the loss is theirs, not yours.

CHAPTER TWO

My Career Begins

In Los Angeles, I found other girls for friends. My new roommate, Vera, came from Norwegian stock, much like me (well, there was also the Swedish from my father and the Danish, Irish, English, Scottish, and Pennsylvania Dutch blood from my mother's side). We were two happy young women ready to conquer the world! We leased an apartment near Los Angeles International Airport (LAX), just a short bus ride away. Our building trembled with noise.

"Holy smokes!" Vera yelled the first time it happened.

"They're gonna land on us!" I answered, ducking.

It turned out we were in the flight path as planes landed every few minutes. We often felt like zombies from lack of sleep, but we eventually adjusted and could snore through the commotion. Sometimes, we stood outside waving to the passengers and pilots as they whooshed by. Around the airport, we became known as the "friendly duo."

As a newcomer to Pan Am, I started with a month of standby duty. Most of my flights were to Hawaii and back. How exciting it was to venture so far from my childhood in Phoenix, pursuing a career that was literally taking me places. I occasionally did a twelve-hour polar flight from LA to London. We provided passengers with drinks, and several courses for lunch, showed a movie, then served tea as we arrived in the British Isles. The last half hour was devoted to collecting trash.

"Where does all this go?" I asked a more experienced crew member.

"In this special little room!" she said as she opened the lavatory door.

She wasn't kidding. We stuffed the trash in there. It was the only place we could find room. These were my first trips as an envoy between two great lands, the U.S and England. My excitement was contagious; passengers and co-workers alike could feel my joy. When you're trying your best, people know it. And they respond. Like the Good Book says, love your neighbor as yourself.

It may sound silly to say this, but if you are likeable, people like you! Pleasantness is one of life's easiest ways to get ahead. When you're feeling particularly sour one day, give smiling a try. People you know may wonder what you're up to … but the people who are new to you, like customers, will enjoy it. Think steppingstone.

I came to love London and the British people. On my very first visit, after a twelve-hour flight, I wanted to explore. Vera, determined to get to the hotel for some sleep, said, "You're crazy! You won't last an hour after a twelve-hour flight!"

I should have listened to her. I walked the streets and looked in shops until I was suddenly weak in the knees and everywhere else. I stumbled into a cab, hustled back to the hotel, and collapsed.

My international travel had begun. I was flying high. And then, because nothing stays the same for very long, a hard decision came my way.

"Susan," Pam Am asked. "Care to fly to Vietnam?"

SIDE-NOTE: Fear Management

Fear is a part of everyone's reality. How you face it is a measure of your strength as a human being.

You will always have it. Fear can save your life if it drives you to take flight from a raging tornado. But it can make your life worth living to take your stand and face down fear on your own terms. Maybe not with fists but with kindness. Maybe not with panic but with control. Maybe not with denial but with boldness. Develop the "tools" that are your strongest allies in life.

As a youngster, I discovered this about myself: learning to hide my fear helped me to control it. It frustrated those bullies on the school bus; by not giving them the pleasure of seeing my dread, they gave up on me.

When we played, my cousins and I never let each other see our fear. If one of us had to descend to the dark of Grampa's basement to use the bathroom down there, each tried to be nonchalant, even though everyone knows basements are full of monsters in coal bins or dragons on the joists above your head.

When an enormous bellowing Holstein bull convinced me that I was his next target, I fled from the barn to the house, slammed through the back door, composed myself, breathed deep, and came into the kitchen with a casual, "What's up, guys?"

Controlling your fear enough to hide it can be a big help, especially once you realize your worries are not particularly special. The only thing unique about them is how you confront them. When fear strikes, I've learned to continue on my assigned course. It gives me the confidence to follow my routine. I've needed that lesson more than once as my career blossomed.

Escaping the Vietcong

I needed to control fear now as I agreed to take the rest and recuperation (R and R) runs in and out of a war zone. We picked up soldiers in Vietnam and delivered them via a refuel stop in Guam to Hawaii. When their leaves were over, we returned them to the war zone.

I did it, if not with glee, at least with a game face and sense of honor. It was war, and it was the right thing to do. This was serious stuff: I was given a card with the rank of 2nd Lieutenant in case I was captured by the enemy.

On one occasion, we were refueling in Cam Ranh Bay, Vietnam. The troops were boarding the plane, and the crew was waiting in a hot little shack beside the runway.

PING! BAM! BLAM!

Gunfire lit up the tarmac! Shots whizzed past us and slammed into our plane. The noise of angry weapons was deafening … and maybe a few of us were screaming as well. It was terrifying.

The captain yelled, "Let's get out of here!"

He didn't have to ask twice. We took off like rabbits, bounding toward the plane as gunfire continued. A crazy memory of running track crossed my mind, but this time I wasn't barefoot; I was in high heels beating my own record nonetheless!

We hustled up the stairs into the plane without too much shoving to get aboard and out of range. Once inside, the crowd was insane. Soldiers were yelling commands and spitting out loud comments regarding the enemy. The plane was packed tight as they clambered to seats and buckled up. On those flights, First Class had been removed so economy seats were nearly wall to wall.

I was petrified, but I remembered my training. It got me through. I looked around and quickly realized someone was missing. It was another stewardess. Monica! The captain had to be told.

I shoved my way to the cockpit, crying, "Captain! Monica is still out there!"

He turned to me, and I saw the fear in his eyes. Surely, he wouldn't leave her behind … he'd go after her!

He surprised me by making it my decision. "Susan, it's your call. I won't ask you to go out there."

All color must have drained from my face. "What do you mean it's my call? You're the captain."

But he didn't offer to do it himself. And there was no time to argue. I'm no hero. But it was one of those moments you make a life-changing decision, and you make it fast. Without another word, I scurried back down the stairs and raced to the shack. Monica was there, frozen in fear. I was trembling as sweat poured down my face. But I took her hand and gave it a tug. That's when she was able to move. Together we tore back to that plane, still under fire. How the bullets missed us, I will never know. It was the scariest moment of my life, but it was also my proudest.

Most of the R and R flights weren't quite so thrilling, thank heaven. We flew soldiers back and forth between Hawaii on the one hand and Cam Ranh Bay, Da Nang, or Saigon on the other. The servicemen were in good spirits at the start of their leave, so we often had fun with them.

A favorite joke was to tell them it would be a topless service. One of us would disappear into the cockpit, so all eyes were glued on that door. Soon a male flight engineer strutted out, no shirt in sight, and began the coffee service. When we could be heard over the general booing, "Hey!" we'd say to the disappointed soldiers. "We promised topless, and we delivered!"

Sometimes we played cards with the men on the galley floor. I still know seven different ways to play poker. If we had a lay-over in Guam, it was twenty guys to every gal at the Top of the Mar Club in the evenings. We danced the night away, always feeling safe and always feeling that these trips were important moments to us then, and to our memories in the future.

So many of these guys were just big kids. Their greatest request of Pan Am was all the fresh cold milk we could carry. The military-issue powered milk was dreaded. Rarely did anyone act anything less than a gentleman. My favorite mishap was an officer who invited me for a boat ride in Guam. Pulling away from the dock, he was bragging that he'd never tip a boat with a pretty girl aboard. Next thing I knew, I was in the water. He'd managed to tip the boat! I've never seen that tone of red on anyone's face since.

SIDE-NOTE: Unattached

You may have noticed that I haven't talked much about the opposite sex. Even though I had my share of boyfriends, there are reasons I didn't form a permanent relationship.

One. I always wanted to be free to follow where life took me next. Starting with that man who said, "I wish I had" in my earliest childhood memories, I was dead set against forming ties that held me back. That included a husband and children.

Two. I rarely stayed in one place long enough for a real relationship to develop, moving from base to base.

Three. The struggle to retain information stayed with me. I spent much of my free time studying. It was necessary for me to excel. I knew my limitation and learned to live with it; you will, too.

Four. I would not be able to keep my job if I married; at that time, stewardesses had to be single to fly.

It was a radical decision in those days, not to have kids. Some small-minded people disapproved. Others thought there was something wrong with me! And all that travel meant no plants or pets, either!

My co-workers were my nearest family during many holidays, in many locations. We gave each other gifts, went to dinner together, and became friends, whether pilot or newest member of the crew. Friendships are life's blessings.

Perks for My Parents

My parents might have wanted grandkids, but they never demanded it. Each took pleasure in my pleasure; they taught me to reach for the sky, and I was doing just that. Plus, they had a couple of nice perks from my career!

Imagine shopping around the world. My first Christmas away from home in 1969 was spent in Hong Kong. What a whirl of bustling people, cars, and rickshaws all zipping in different directions. I bought shoes, a handbag, and a suit for my mom, plus a beautiful sports jacket for my dad with his name embroidered inside. In addition to gifts from foreign ports, I was able to provide my parents with tickets to the world as my career expanded.

Our first trip together was a vacation to Scandinavia. We were some of the first in our family in America to go back since my grandparents had immigrated. Our plane out of New York was a jam-packed Boeing 707. You could hardly move in your seat and getting down the aisle was out of the question without sucking in your breath. We were tired from misadventures getting to the plane (abusive taxi driver, forgotten passport, late departure, need I go on?), but a jolly group of Russians kept us awake with their celebration long into the wee hours.

We were more than ready to deplane at our stop in Copenhagen, but the city was fogged in, so the plane diverted to Hamburg, Germany. I groaned to myself; I really wanted this trip to be a joy for Mom, Dad, and me. In Hamburg, we faced a six-hour train ride back to Copenhagen, where we missed our connection to Bornholm, Denmark. I wondered just how much my folks were liking this gift of travel. A gentleman in charge of operations with Pan Am found us a good room for the night. I will be eternally grateful.

In the morning, the city was socked in again. We decided a boat to Bornholm was our best bet, although it didn't leave Copenhagen till evening. Nonetheless, it was a good call because the weather remained dour. The boat was an overnight ride, and by the time we stuffed ourselves into our little cabin, we were exhausted. The three of us fell into a deep stupor. When the boat arrived in port the next morning, we missed all calls that we had arrived. A steward had to come wake us up and shoo us off the boat.

Our relatives had gathered on the dock to meet us. They nearly gave up their vigil when, at last, a trio of bleary-eyed Americans was booted off. My mom's cousin dismissed our apologies with a laugh. "You didn't wake up because they knocked on your door in Danish!"

Bornholm was important to us because it was where my mother's father had been born. We spent a couple of days there, visiting my grandfather's old home and eating so much we thought we would burst. Our family, maybe like yours, celebrates love with food. Finally, we waddled onto a boat to Stockholm, where we rented a car to visit more family in Stenberga, Sweden, and Toten, Norway. Even though the trip got off to a rough start, I saw firsthand how caring and hard-working Scandinavians are. I flew away home, very proud of my heritage.

CHAPTER THREE

Leaving LA for NY

After six months in Los Angeles, I decided to give New York a try. It was the largest east coast base for Pan Am. Other than Chicago, all the bases in the US were on the coasts, and each offered different cultures and opportunities.

In New York, I applied for the position of Purser. Pan Am called their planes Clippers and used many nautical terms. A purser on a ship was the officer in charge of money matters. Other airlines call the position Head Flight Attendant.

It was a position of prestige that came with extra pay, more authority, and my own hotel room. Applying meant more training and a white-knuckle check flight as a final test. On a two-hour flight from JFK to Freeport, Bahamas, I had to complete a First-Class Service (I remember it to this day … roast beef cart, cheese cart, dessert cart, and more). In addition, I counted the liquor sales from the Economy Class, where mini bottles were sold, and I completed the necessary paperwork, compiling deposits from all the different currencies on board. My first task off the plane was to deposit the money, all balanced. If I didn't complete these tasks, I would fail. If I succeeded, it was assumed I could do any flight.

I messed up one thing. Instead of calmly announcing, "Please extinguish all cigarettes," I was so excited, I said, "all smoking material." My check purser said it sounded like the plane was on fire! I was forgiven, I survived, and I became a purser.

This was another time my perseverance was not appreciated by one and all. The New York base had many stewardesses with far more experience than me. They didn't want to be pursers because it would affect their seniority, but they weren't interested in answering to a rookie, either. As with the women from training school, I just had to suck it up and ignore any arrows coming my way. In time, I won them over by recognizing their professionalism. They knew what they were doing; they didn't need me to micromanage. I respected them, and vice versa.

Seeing the World

From New York, I was introduced to much of Europe as well as Africa and South America. I flew regularly scheduled flights as well as charters. I loved the German countryside and scrumptious food (one baker's strudel rivaled my gramma's cookies for top billing in my heart). But Germany also introduced me to harsh concepts of war that were new to me. I was exploring Cologne when I came across a cathedral, bombed in World War II and left in ruins as a reminder. It has stuck with me for decades, so I guess it achieved its goal. I also found Berlin cold, especially during the wall years. Checkpoint Charlie was spooky. East Berliners didn't laugh or look up to your face. It made me appreciate the sunny way I had grown up, safe from the specter of war in my hometown. What a different person I might be if that had been the case.

I spent time in Moscow studying the Russian language for Pan Am. I found it a beautiful city with wonderful people and blinis (Russian pancakes) to die for, but it could be another nerve-wracking part of the world.

I was walking on a free afternoon when a child approached me. "Chewing gum, lady?" he asked. This may have been the extent of his English. I had been told before I went that the kids there were delighted by a good chew, so I had some in my purse. When I gave him a pack, his huge grin was my reward.

No sooner had I walked away when I felt a hand like an enormous claw descend on my shoulder. A big man pulled me into an alley, threw me up against a wall, and flashed his KGB badge.

"What are you doing?" he yelled. "You are destroying the teeth of our children. It is forbidden to give them chewing gum."

My life flashed before me. I was certain I'd never see my family, friends, or home again. But I remembered my lesson about controlling fear, and I spoke up in a manner to protect the child. "Oh, how stupid of *me*. I am so sorry. I didn't know."

"Well, don't ever do it again." He released my collar and walked away. I shook like a leaf as I stood there, trying to regain my composure before I scurried on. To this day, I never carry chewing gum!

SIDE-NOTE: You Can Conquer It

While I think most of us can overcome our backgrounds, I certainly understand that the odds are tougher for some. I had my share of teachers who weren't happy if we weren't miserable, but I had great ones, too. One remains dear to me to this day; Mrs. Suter was my fifth-grade teacher who saw me through those wretched fractions. She must have wanted to throw the textbook in exasperation, but she never did. With her gentle patience, I learned. It was persistence that she taught me, modeled on her own. Thanks, Mrs. Suter, for being there and being a very dear friend.

While special teachers are important, nothing rivals good parents. I had a "Beaver Cleaver" childhood with far more love than punishment. It was one long lesson in the positives of life, interspersed with the fun of drive-in movies, cold chocolate milk on hot Phoenix days, family picnics, and horseback rides. It's important to know you have someone who cares about you. To realize there are children with parents who don't care, abuse them mentally or physically … well, that is an abomination. I cannot fathom the sad fact that people bring children into this world to abandon them. If this is your situation, your journey will be harder than some. Yet, I cannot stress enough that you can overcome adversity for a happy, fulfilled life. Believe you are deserving of love. You are important. Never think overwise. Success awaits you in the trying. You can flourish. I have worked with people who suffered a stepfather's beatings, a mother's alcoholism, and an eviction from the family. It is easy for these people to stop growing, to become callous, unfriendly, and negative. They excel at making life dismal for those around them, and that almost guarantees them continued failure in their own endeavors. Avoid this trap for yourself. Break the habits of your background, and escape to a healthy, productive life. And for those of us who have had great families, try to realize there are those who don't. It took me a long time to understand why someone was so hurtful toward me. It wasn't personal, but due to their bitterness. Tolerance can be a great gift. To this day, I am still trying to learn that lesson.

The Rest of the World

I went everywhere and soaked up every experience I could get. This was the main benefit I derived from doing the job of a stewardess. People everywhere liked meeting a woman who liked meeting them. Never be too cool or standoffish to learn what is offered around you. And if there is one thing I learned in traveling the world, it is that regardless of where you are from or what language you speak, we all have the desire to be needed and loved. It is currency you can bank; every employer wants not only knowledgeable employees but also understanding ones when handling customers.

A month of charter flights to Malaga, Spain, one October, was a lovely treat where the hotel was on the beach. From Nice, I caught a train to see the Palace of Monaco in Monte Carlo, then on to Rome. Even back then, the traffic was horrendous, and your derriere was likely to be pinched if you didn't step lively. As I became more senior, I had more opportunities, such as a ten-day tour of Africa: Accra, Lagos, Monrovia, Entebbe, Dakar, and Nairobi. In that latter location, I managed a photographic safari.

Thailand and India were fountains of treasure. In Bangkok, a jewelry shop called Smiley's was awash with 18-karat gold and Cambodian green jade. We visited the Taj Mahal in India, which is quite a sight, but the country's poverty was haunting. Once in New Delhi, we arrived at three in the morning. On our way to the hotel, we saw a cart moving along the street, picking up bodies of the diseased and neglected who had died in the night.

Far to the north, I explored my maternal grandmother's ancestral homes of Scotland and Ireland. If it is blarney that you're needing, then Ireland is the spot for you.

"Top of the mornin' to you," said a short, old man in a crusty brogue as I made my way up the worn, narrow steps of Blarney Castle. "Would you be wanting to kiss the Blarney Stone?"

"Yes, I would," I replied.

"Well then, follow me."

We made our way up another set of stairs that brought us to the castle's roof.

"Now, you'll be needing to lie down on your back with your head hanging over the side." It had to be nearly one hundred feet down to the ground. "I'll hold on to your feet, and you can kiss the stone overhead."

I couldn't believe it. This gent could never hold my feet. I'd join the pile of stones far below. Nonetheless, I couldn't refuse him. And, sure enough, the Irishman was plenty strong for the job. I kissed the Blarney Stone, and I guess it did give me the gift of gab … at least enough to write it down in this book!

Back to Bornholm

I had the opportunity to visit my relatives in Bornholm again during a layover in Copenhagen. However, the plane was small, and every seat was taken.

Since I was a stewardess when I was on duty, I was allowed to hitch a ride in the cockpit. The captain and co-pilot were in their seats by the time I squeezed into the tiny space and crouched behind them. I saw no seat for me.

"Come on in, and close the door," the pilot said.

"Wait a minute, guys," I replied, crossing my arms. "I know Scandinavians are hospitable, but sitting on one of your laps is getting a little carried away, don't you think?"

They both grinned, and the captain quipped, "That would be fine by us, but it's against regulations. You'll have to sit in your own seat." He pointed to the door behind me. Hanging on it was what looked like a cushion dangling from a strap. I figured no guts, no glory … belted myself on to that precarious pull-down perch … and with no more ceremony, we were soon racing down the runway. My knees were propped between the pilots, and my knuckles turned white as I grasped the backs of their seats. The entire instrument panel was shaking as much as my knees! I closed my eyes as I saw my life flash before me. I hadn't been this scared since Vietnam.

When I staggered off that plane in Bornholm, my relatives gasped. "You look like you've seen a ghost."

"Worse than that," I said. "I've seen death streaking by."

In the days to come, I took my parents with me to Australia and New Zealand. Heading further north, I visited Tahiti and Bali. Our crew rented bikes to see the islands. We always managed to find the fun.

Once in Manilla, we found delicious mangoes for sale in the market, twelve for a dollar. When we got back aboard to head for Honolulu, we learned that Customs wouldn't allow fruit brought to the US, so the crew pooled our mangoes and served eight dozen to the passengers. I had flowers in my room in Beirut, was served breakfast on a Mediterranean balcony, rode a camel in Damascus (a hilarious experience with one of the few animals I'd be happy to never see again), fed my inner chocoholic in the Switzerland Alps, then lived for several months with a family in England when based in London.

It was life-changing, the international travel, a dream come true. I've seen and tried so many new things. You can, too. Don't let anyone make you believe you can't.

SIDE-NOTE: To Be Free, You Must Stay Free

Women have not always been encouraged to network and support each other. We haven't always learned how to manage money, and that can put you so far behind an eight-ball you may never get free of bad breaks. Learn to do it yourself; financial freedom is a major part of personal freedom. Get as much education as you can. Be secure in your own abilities in case a relationship doesn't work out.

So many young women have babies too soon. Give yourself time to discover what you really want before you take that irretraceable step. Once a baby arrives, your options are vastly limited. Hold off until you can take care of yourself and a child while you pursue the other things that make your life as happy as it's meant to be.

PART III
LIFE IN TRANSITION

CHAPTER ONE

A Change of Pace

When I was little, I never actually toddled. I kept crawling, even after I could walk because it was faster. From crawling, I skipped right to running. I could often be seen galloping in circles through the house, putting on the brakes to take a sip of milk waiting on a kitchen shelf, and then running down the sidewalk to meet my dad when he came home from work.

I suppose that sort of set the pace for my entire life. If something new came along that "felt right," I was all for giving it a go. I had seen a great deal of the world, in fact, I felt like an ambassador in my own right. But I was still determined to work my way into the foreign service. And so, I transferred to Pan Am's base in

Washington D.C. to be closer to the center of all things governmental.

SIDE-NOTE: A Dirty Word

I've never liked the word "failure." To me, it's the real curse word. True failure is to not try. If you don't try, you fail yourself, not society. Only you can live your life. You have everything to gain if you try what interests you. Regardless of the outcome, you are a success (assuming you aren't trying for an addiction or committing a crime). Don't put yourself in the position of looking back on your life and saying, "I wish I had."

Moving to Washington D.C.

I reported to Dulles International Airport on December 28, 1972. As the bus from the airport made its way through the city, all I could think about was how I was in my nation's capital. Here, the President resided, Congress made laws, and the Supreme Court upheld the constitutionality of those laws. This was where it all happened, and I'd be right in the heart of it. It was like living history to be in Washington, D.C.

I planned to stay at the YWCA in downtown D.C. until I found an apartment. As it turned out, I stayed there for almost five years, only leaving because the building was to be torn down to make way for a new high rise. The Y was such a great location. My bus to the airport was just around the corner, the White House was only four blocks away, and Capitol Hill was within walking distance. Having some days between flights, I decided to volunteer up on the Hill to gain some government experience.

I worked as a congressional aide for several offices, but my favorite post took me back to a childhood hero. Senator Barry Goldwater (US Air Force Officer, five-term senator, author, and businessman) was virtually a legend in Arizona. I'd first met the senator while I was still in high school. My speech teacher, Miss Salisbury, arranged for me to meet with him regarding the air pollution in Phoenix (a panel I was doing for my class). He and his son had recently published a book on the subject. After discussing the problem, he invited me for a flight in his private plane to see where this all started. There is no doubt this kind man piqued my curiosity about politics and the world at large.

I met him again when I was on the International Relations Board for ASU. I was taking a group of Brazilian students on a tour of Phoenix. Before returning to the campus, I asked the students if they would like to meet Senator Goldwater. At his home, the Senator invited the students into his Ham Radio building, putting them in touch with their families back in Brazil.

Now, many years later, I had a chance to return Senator Goldwater's faith in me by becoming an aide.

"Susan," he asked me one day. "Do you like Mexican food?"

"Do I ever!" At that time, you couldn't get any in Washington.

"Me, too. I'm going to have Jordan's send us a plane full of food, so let me know your schedule next month."

Jordan's Mexican Food was a fantastic restaurant in downtown Phoenix. Senator Goldwater treated his whole staff plus the staff of the other Arizona Senator and two Congressmen, to a feast. We felt like we'd gone to heaven. I'd had wonderful meals all over the world by that point in my life, but nothing tasted as good as home.

CHAPTER TWO

The Nation's Business

I became invested in national politics as well as international. Pan Am helped pique that interest. For instance, one night soon after he left office, I had Spiro Agnew in first-class from London to Washington. Pan Am had upstairs service on the 747, where he and eleven guests dined. Afterward, they returned downstairs to watch a movie. I cleaned up and sat to have my own lunch.

The former vice president appeared at the top of the stairs. "Hello, Susan," he said. "Would you mind if I joined you?"

"Of course not, Mr. Vice President. I would be honored if you don't mind my eating in front of you."

"Not at all."

I could tell he wanted to get away from the people downstairs. We talked for a good hour about our families.

Another adventure, courtesy of Pan Am: President Nixon's wife, Pat, asked if some of us could serve on the presidential yacht, *USS Sequoia*. Mrs. Nixon was a frequent hostess to Vietnam veterans for burger lunches aboard as we cruised the Potomac.

The Press Corps

I was honored to be selected to work the Presidential press flights during the Ford administration. At that time, there was no room for the press on Air Force One because it wasn't a 747. So, the President was on one 707, and the press corps flew on another. It was exciting to meet the top news reporters and anchormen of the day. Their jobs left them little time for home and family, so I could easily relate.

In Philadelphia, I met President Ford. He was hosting a fundraiser for Governor Scranton. Members of the press were required to stay in a roped-off area. I decided that didn't apply to *me*. After all, I wasn't press! I told them I was going to the President's table to take a picture.

"You're crazy! …You'll never get past the rope … the Secret Service will stop you," the press harped as one.

"Oh yeah? Watch me." Away I went, under the rope, past the Secret Service, up to the head table, and up to President Ford.

"Hello, Mr. President. May I take a picture?"

He laughed and said, "Anything for Miss Pan Am."

Did I ever gloat, strutting back to the media area to receive handshakes and pats on the back. Then I had to sit before I collapsed. I guess this tale goes under the heading of It Never Hurts to Ask.

SIDE-NOTE: Flexibility

If you can be as light on your feet with your career as Muhammed Ali was with his, you are halfway to success. Make a plan, sure. Work it, of course. But when a better idea comes along, a superior strategy, a goal that fits better, well, don't be afraid to snap it up. As I said earlier, opportunities aren't always easy to recognize, and you need to stay flexible to be open to them.

Time to Consider and Reconsider

I began to question if being a stewardess was right for me any longer. I had spoken with Georgetown University about their master's program in Foreign Studies; but in truth? It was too expensive for a working girl whose commitment was wavering. I knew, with my studying shortcomings, I'd be at it forever. I wanted to *do,* not sit in a classroom.

I thought about it long and hard. I asked the advice of foreign service people I trusted. They told me I had done more as an ambassador for the US than they did. One said, "I sit in an embassy stamping passports all day. You are out meeting people."

I began to give other options a try … things I could do while still employed as a purser. I even volunteered as a Reserve Officer with the D.C. Metropolitan Police Department, attending the police academy and qualifying with a .38 revolver. I never carried the gun on active duty, but my uniform was identical to the regular officers, so I heard my share of verbal abuse and ripe obscenities. It was a perilous job; danger lurked around corners. While I respected the officers, I realized that living under threat was not high on my To-Do list. I'd had fearful experiences of my own flying for Pan Am.

Close Calls

There were only three times since my experience in Vietnam a decade earlier that I felt peril on the big jets. Once, on the way from Los Angeles to Hawaii, we lost three engines. I was working in economy when I heard a thump. I called the cockpit and was informed we'd lost oil to one of the engines. Moments later, I heard another loud thump. Yes, it was another engine.

The captain assured me that 747s could fly with only two engines. Sure. I'd still prefer all four. Fortunately, we were in sight of land when the third quit. On only one remaining engine, we landed safe and sound. That's how I know how great the 747s were.

At Heathrow, we were taxiing to the runway when a man leaped from his seat and ran towards me. I jumped up, yelling, "What's wrong?"

"I have to get off this plane *now*!" he gasped.

"Okay, okay, just a moment," I said as calmly as I could, as visions of hijacking danced in my head. I called the cockpit. "Captain, we have a man who wants off the plane right now." I listened a second, then said to the man, "We're on our way back to the terminal."

The tower put us on the tarmac in case of any bombs. Security personnel with rifles boarded the plane, escorting the man away. Everything was taken off the plane to check for a bomb, but none was found. Six hours later, we were on our way … I never did learn what happened to the guy. That may be just as well!

On another flight, invisible turbulence caused us to drop 5,000 feet. It was terrifying. The cockpit had received word from control that the plane ahead of us was reporting rough air. The captain required passengers to take their seats and buckle up. Soon after, he ordered the crew to do the same.

Of course, the passengers were trying to eat! And I was in the back, surrounded by mini bottles of alcohol I was inventorying. Nonetheless, I dropped everything and hustled to my jump seat as ordered.

WHAM! The plane dropped. Everything not tied down went airborne, including trays, food, miniatures, luggage, and worst of all, passengers who hadn't bothered to heed the seat belt warnings.

One man flew across the aisle and hit his head on the metal edge of my jump seat. He had a huge gash and was bleeding profusely. His wife began shrieking, "He's dead" repeatedly.

"He's not dead," I tried and failed to calm her." I managed to grab one of the mini bottles, opened it, and poured its contents over the man's head. It's all I could think to do for the wound at that moment.

The captain called me again. "Susan, will you go through the cabin and count the injured so we know how many ambulances we need in New York."

"Of course." I unbuckled my seatbelt, which was scary.

"Be careful. Crawl, don't walk. We may encounter another drop."

Now, that was seriously scary. But I'd flown with this captain several times and trusted his judgment. I lowered to my hands and knees and began the long crawl. The aisles were full of possessions, food, and trash, but I kept on. Many passengers were weeping in terror. But soon, they began calling out to me how many were injured in their rows. Those who could, reached out to pat me. Oh, how important is human touch in hours like this!

When I made it back to my jump seat, I called the captain. We had twenty injured in a plane that looked like a tornado had whirled through the cabin. I know I was in shock because I kept worrying about the mess for the clean-up crew.

CHAPTER THREE

Spreading My Wings

The day came when I knew exactly what I wanted to do next. I just woke up knowing! I didn't want to just ride in a plane. I wanted to fly one!

I began hanging around the cockpit right behind the captain for take-offs and landings. I listened to the tower on the earphones. When passengers were asleep, I talked with the engineer, co-pilot, or captain (whoever wasn't busy at the moment). I learned what each lever did, and what every gadget was for. Yes, I was a pest. You be one, too … learn everything you can from the people who are doing what you want to do.

I took classes from the FAA Flying Club. My instructor, Skip, was a character to be sure, but he could really fly. I soloed and cross-countried without crashing (I did nearly run out of gas once, but let's keep that to ourselves). I received my private pilot certification on April 20, 1976. I was a full-fledged pilot!

Of course, the next day I was back in the air as a stewardess. However, I can reveal all these years later, the captain of the 747 I served on? He jumped out of his seat and told me to take the controls.

"But I fly a Cessna 172, not a Boeing 747!"

"It's all the same," the captain said. And he must have been right. At least nobody in those passenger compartments knew I was the person in the captain's seat, flying that magnificent machine for fifteen minutes.

I was ready. I'd enjoyed my life as a stewardess, but it was time for the next phase in my life. I prepared to jump to the next steppingstone.

Fate Steps In

And then it was 1977, a crummy year for me. I had to move to new digs, even though I loved living at the Y. I had to break up with a man I had admired and knew I would miss. And I developed a dermoid cyst on my left ovary.

In order to remove the cyst, the surgeon had to remove the ovary. That complex surgery kept me out of work for two months. When I could return to my job, my heart was no longer in it. I said good-bye to Pan Am after a wonderful decade of international travel and making friendships I have till this day.

I didn't exactly have a complete plan in place. But I had a thought. *If I can fly fixed wing planes, why not helicopters?*

Why not, indeed?

PART IV
YOU'RE IN THE ARMY NOW

Susan Strand front row, center.

CHAPTER ONE

Waiting For the Military to Move

At the Y, I had seen a recruitment poster for the Coast Guard. A helicopter was hovering over the Potomac dangling a brave man below who was rescuing a poor soul from the water. Wow! What an image that planted in my brain. It took root and began to grow.

I would like to help people that brave to do their jobs. I could already fly a plane. Why not learn the complexities of flying a helicopter? Anyone old enough to remember Vietnam had become an admirer of the crews who flew these cantankerous beasts.

It could be dangerous, sure. My uncle, along with many other military pilots, called them eggbeaters, whirlybirds, catapults, or nicknames too colorful to print here. Maybe I was crazy. Or maybe I had learned to deal with fear. Either way, I was ready to go.

But this was 1978, and the Army wasn't ready for me. Women weren't allowed to be helicopter pilots. The recruiter rejected me no matter how much I pestered.

"Ma'am! We don't take women in flight school," he said in frustration.

"Oh., yeah?" I answered, my frustration oversizing his. "THAT'S GONNA CHANGE, BUDDY!"

And change it did. This time in our history was a growth period for women's rights. Our abilities to handle roles formally closed to us could no longer be overlooked; cracks were appearing in old beliefs. I merely needed to bide my time. I took a job at an aeronautical school in Florida and awaited the call. Meanwhile, I battled it out with cockroaches that were nearly the size of ponies. Welcome to the wetlands, right? I adopted a stray cat to help with that issue. Other than that, I liked my job, and my landlords, and I was prepared to wait for the Army to come to its senses.

It did, and just a few months after my move to the Southland, the Army decided to accept women into flight school. A big push in that direction came from a very fine Air Force colonel at the Pentagon, Colonel Glasebrook. He had taken an interest in my qualifications and refused to give up even after several attempts by the Army to keep me out.

The next barrier was my age. The upper limit was twenty-seven, and I was thirty-three. That ceiling shattered, too, a little later in the year.

SIDE-NOTE: Patience Is More Than a Virtue

Any good hunter or fisherman will tell you that patience is part of the process. You cramp up hunkered in a duck blind or freeze in a trout stream. Think of opportunity the same way. Sometimes you catch the trophy by waiting it out.

When you decide to modify a goal, you better take the long view. Consider how life-changing a new direction might be. Think through the obstacles … can you handle the extra education, the commute, the travel, the cut in pay, the reduced title, and all the other downsides that can come along with a career change?

If you can, do it. It's your life; sometimes, you must put yourself on pause long enough to gather your wits for a life shift. Your new goal may not be ready for you until you take another course or learn a previously unneeded skill. I learned I didn't want to be a cop by volunteering as a reserve officer. You may do something similar.

Don't become a nurse if you discover you panic at the sight of blood!

Prepare to take a step back in pay and title when you make your move. It's all part of persevering. There will be others with better qualifications than you if they've been at it a while … or younger than you if they're just starting out. You must pass them with your willingness to learn and your enthusiasm for the job. Any employer or HR expert can sniff out the person who truly wants the job and is best qualified for it.

Be patient. You need it to prepare for a future that aligns with the person you are now.

Old Lady Strand

Let me repeat. I would be thirty-three among other recruits still in their teens. I moved back to Phoenix to begin a regimen to build my strength against the day I entered the Army. My "commanding officer" was my dad, who remembered his own basic training from WWII.

He began by filling a backpack with rocks. "Climb," he said, pointing toward a 2600-foot Phoenix Mountain now called Piestewa Peak. "Build up your strength and endurance."

Good grief! The heat, the sweat, the whimpering, and suffering! But Dad was right. I got stronger in less time than you'd think possible.

"Now run," he commanded. "Fleet as an antelope. You go, girl!"

I started with a quarter-turn around a big school track. Phew! It wore me out Day One. I kept at it until I could do eight full circles.

A former school principal of mine stopped me one day to ask what I was doing. When I told him, he said that in the Navy during the war, they had to scurry across jungle gym bars.

I climbed the one at the school and grabbed hold. I struggled to the first bar. There I dangled, unable to make another move. Finally, like a ripe fruit, I dropped to the ground. Hmm. This was going to take more out of me than I thought. I did, finally, conquer the beast. I won't say I was a natural, but I could get my crate from one end to the other without an embarrassing stop in the middle. I was as ready as I was going to get.

But the Army still balked. They seemed to keep losing my papers. Finally, I connected with a female captain in a main recruiting office. Within four hours, she got back to me with a start date for basic training followed by flight school.

I think about her now and then; how she cut through the red tape for me. How she was determined to help another determined female candidate. How hard her own climb must have been. If you ask me, I say be prepared to help others in life. Be particularly prepared to go to bat for other women you think could excel.

CHAPTER TWO

Fort Leonard Wood

After another physical, more paperwork, and swearing in, I said good-bye to my parents and joined four other recruits – all male - headed from Phoenix to Fort Leonard Wood, Missouri. A huge bus rumbled out of the darkness to pick us up where we huddled on the tarmac. A stern voice called to us, "Get on and make it snappy." Was that menacing growl really the voice of Uncle Sam?

We hustled aboard. It was dark inside. None of us got the best seat because there *were* no seats. We hung on straps like so many subway riders.

It was ten at night when I was dropped at the women's barracks which looked like something right out of a black and white movie. It was filled with cots that were filled with snoring bodies. The matron took me upstairs and blurted gruffly, "You'll sleep here." I collapsed into deep sleep.

A blaring bugle blasted me out of bed. "Out of bed, you good-for-nothing lazy bones!" followed the bugle. "Shower and get outside in ten minutes."

A stampede of women hit the latrines all at once. I made it out front on time but admit I'd barely splashed my face. Somebody barked at us. "Hurry up. Lineup. Look lively. Face me. Stand straight. Stomach in. Chest out." It was like a flak attack to the brain! "I'm your drill sergeant, and for the next eight weeks you will obey me and your platoon leader. STRAND! Front and center!"

What on earth had I done wrong all ready? "He...here I am, Drill Sergeant. I'm Strand."

"Take charge of this platoon on the double."

What? He must be mistaken. "Me, Sir?" I squeaked.

"Yes, you. And don't call me sir. Officers are sir. I'm Drill Sergeant."

I leaped into action, trying to herd twenty-five women into some sort of order as we followed the drill sergeant to the supply depot to pick up our gear. I felt the way an inexperienced sheepdog must feel on her first day with the flock. Except none of these sheep were the least bit scared of me.

With our gear, we "marched" to another barracks, a far newer one than the night before. As the others began choosing beds, the drill sergeant said, "Strand. Come with me."

I didn't want to go. I wanted to stake out my bed. I wanted to ignore him.

I went on the double.

He explained my duties as I stood in front of his desk. He chose me for platoon leader no doubt because I was about twice the age of the other recruits. Maybe he thought I'd mother them. Boy, did he have the wrong picture.

"Drill Sergeant, I have no idea what I'm doing. You should reconsider."

"Nope."

Was that it? End of discussion?

Then he unwound a bit. "If you're going to be an officer, you need to be a leader. You can handle it. I'm here to help you." Somehow some of my paperwork must have gotten to him. He seemed to know what I planned. Almost kindly, he added, "Now let's get you settled."

He gave me a room of my own. My dad would be amazed … or was this a different army than he'd told me about?

"Now go see how your platoon is settling in," he said. I was feeling pretty cocky on my way to my own platoon. This wasn't so bad after all.

They disliked me immediately. Eyes stared daggers: their disapproval and jealousy reverberated around the room.

Okay, we'll play it that way, I thought.

Instead of a friendly howdy, I squared my shoulders and barked, "My name is Susan Strand, and I am your platoon leader. My room is down the hall. The door will always be open. I'm here to help and want us to be friendly, but don't forget; I'm second in command to the drill sergeant. I expect you to do what I ask with no backtalk."

Two girls came up to me immediately. "Oh yeah?" the mouthier one said. "We ain't gonna take nothin' from you."

I knew I'd have to keep an eye on this streetwise duet. But for now, I ignored them and yelled over their shoulders, "Stow your gear. The drill sergeant will be in shortly to show us how to make the beds." I turned to go stow my own gear but came face to face with the drill sergeant.

"What she says, goes. You have any problems, see her. She reports to me. Understood?"

"Yes, Drill Sergeant," came a collective meek reply.

"I can't hear you!"

"YES, DRILL SERGEANT."

He definitely had our attention. We made beds so tight you couldn't begin to get into one. Then he ordered me to follow him once again.

Fortunately, he just gave me a bit more advice before releasing me. I was tired, still had to put my gear away, and wanted a shower. I entered the room to the sound of all women griping.

"Who does he think he is?"

"That Army recruiter lied to me. I thought I could do what I want."

When one spotted me, the complaints came my way. "Here comes teacher's pet."

"Must be nice to order us around."

"And have your own room."

I marched in robe and flip-flops to the center of the pack. "I didn't ask for this job, but since I have it, we're going to be one of the best platoons around. And we're going to do it together." I was shaking like a leaf, praying it didn't show. I shouted even louder, "Army means team. The more we work together, the easier it will be on all of us."

I noticed that even the two who'd told me to shove off wore shocked expressions. Hoping they'd all hit the sack before they rebelled —and actually give teamwork a thought—I made a beeline for the showers.

My wake-up call at four a.m. was my drill sergeant pounding on my door, yelling, "Strand!!! Get those gals down to formation on the double."

I shot up like a rocket (a very sleepy rocket). "Ye…yes, sir." *Where the heck am I?* I thought in shock. *Oh yes: I'm in the Army now!* "Um … I mean Drill Sergeant!!"

I flew from my room, and all I could see were women flapping and circling like chickens with their heads cut off. They were squawking, and soon, I was screaming louder than any of them. "Get the lead out! Formation in five minutes." I was no longer wondering where I was, but *who* I was. I'd become a tough nut not to be trifled with. At least, I sounded like one.

Learning to Lead

Basic training involves marching, marching, and when you are done, marching some more. Before leaving home, my dad gave me two pointers: 1) never volunteer; 2) be sure and get boots that fit. After several visits to supply, they finally gave me a pair of men's boots for my big feet, and that did the trick. Nonetheless, they had to be broken in. We all had Dr. Scholl's moleskin in every nick and corner of our boots. We made Dr. Scholl a rich man; the same was true for the guy who invented athlete's foot powder. The saddle soap folks did okay, too, as we muscled away with polishing cloths to keep footwear sparkling, even in the deepest folds.

I marshaled my platoon together to be shot with air guns on both sides as we were immunized against virtually every known virus, disease, and then some. The whole platoon moaned with bloody arms.

The physical training was brutal, but I excelled due to the good program my dad had devised for me. I thought about him a lot in those early days of physical and mental duress. He'd been a soldier in WWII and had experienced the endless hardships of those years. I could pick up my feet a little higher and run a few more laps a little faster whenever I thought about him. I motivated my platoon by doing more than I asked them to do, like running with them around the track after I'd done my laps and more push-ups and sit-ups. "Come on, you bag of lazy bones!" I'd yell. "You can do it." And more than once, through all the trials, I kept going by thanking my father for his service.

A leadership role is not always easy. During maneuvers, one of the women was terrified of swinging across a creek on a rope. I yelled and cajoled. "Don't be a sissy! Everyone else did it." Well, she tried all right. She swung BAM into the riverbank, breaking her leg. She hadn't known enough to lift her legs as she approached. I caused that injury because I assumed; I didn't explain it to her. It was my responsibility. She never did learn, but she had reason for her pride. She became the sharpest shooter in the group. She was proud, and so was I.

Night maneuvers under real fire were scary. I asked John Wayne to join my father in my imagination. Together we survived without casualties, me yelling, "Keep down and keep moving. Let's go. Charge!"

SIDE-NOTE: Leading Isn't Everything

Not everyone is cut out to be a leader, and that's not a bad thing. If you don't want the responsibility, then be part of the pack. But be the best part.

Don't hide behind the others. Go ahead and shine. Let it be known that you are a dependable soldier, one that will never let her side down. Stand a little taller, move a little faster, and help a little more. Be the go-to when management needs the one person who can accomplish nearly any task at hand.

This kind of motivation is a skill impossible to teach. Oh, a boss can create an environment in which people want to be motivated. But she can't give you the drive, smarts, and desire it takes to dig in and succeed. You bring that to the party with you.

Stand out as the one who gets things done. There's an old saying: if you are dependable, people will depend on you. True enough. And it feels great.

Graduation

For the first time, we were allowed to peel off our fatigues in favor of dress uniforms. We even donned nylons, high heels, and make-up. The men in the other three companies didn't recognize us! And despite our bickering, we had become a family through the pain, suffering, and hardships of basic training.

One drill sergeant was always selected for having the best platoon. What a shock when they announced our platoon had done it. Our guy beamed with pride. "Strand," he said to me, "I couldn't have done it without you."

And then the big surprise. The two women who'd given me such a hard time in the early going, were standing there. "Thanks, Susan," said one. With a hug, the other said, "You've been the best friend we've ever had."

After a few rounds of "For She's a Jolly Good Fellow," we all went our separate ways. I wonder where they are now. As for me, I was transported to Fort Rucker, Alabama, home to helicopter training for most of the services.

I was going to be a helicopter pilot. Wow.

PART V
HELICOPTER PILOT

Pilot Strand readies a commercial
helicopter for lift off

CHAPTER ONE

Officer Development Training

Fort Rucker covers over 60,000 acres of Alabama countryside. I lugged my gear through the door of my new barracks, which held sixty people. Fifty-eight were men in a dorm-like setting. The other woman and I had a room with a lock on it.

The sixty of us were roused at four a.m. which is apparently the Army's favorite time of day. Our Tactical Officer (TAC) took us to an area where we did sit-ups and push-ups, then ran three miles. We were going to collapse, if we'd had the guts.

"Now hit the showers," our TAC officer yelled.

The other woman and I, both dripping in sweat, stared wide-eyed at each other. The problem? Men and women shared one latrine!

"Girls first. You've got two minutes," our leader added.

We flew into the showers without the aid of a flying machine. As we scrubbed, we could hear the men outside the latrine door taunting us to hurry up. Women in flight school was a brand-new concept and not one with which everyone agreed.

Our sixty exhausted WOCS (Warrant Officer Candidates) piled into a disheveled, heavy-breathing formation after showering.

The TAC officer frowned at us. "Numb skulls, all of you. Baked beans! You call this a formation? You look like something the cat dragged in."

I wish the cat would drag me back to bed, I thought, tired enough to faint.

Walking down the ranks, our TAC officer kindly pointed out poorly shined boots, loose threads on garments, wrinkled fatigues, and loose buttons. Each fault earned you a demerit; twenty-three demerits in a week meant no weekend time off for you. Arggh!

We were hungry as a pack of wolves. But we had to "cross the bars" first. The TAC officer said with disdain, "You girls can do push-ups instead."

Darn it! I could do anything the men could do. I'd practiced back in Phoenix for this. Who was this TAC guy to tell me I can't? While the other female hit the ground for push-ups, I squeaked, "Sir. May I do the bars?"

Picture a big man staring down at the little woman, each taking the other's measure. We must have looked like a cartoon of determination.

"Okay, Strand. Do your stuff." I could tell he thought I'd made a big mistake.

At that moment, I heard my childhood classmates cheering the way they did when I won that Good Sportsmanship Award. I heard my father egging me on. With that audience behind me, I did it; I crossed the bars.

Finally, the whole batch of us could eat. But even that had its issues. Officer development training meant for the first week, you ate your meals "square." You couldn't look at your tray and had to keep your eyes front. You brought your utensil straight up, over to your mouth, then back out and straight down. There was a reason for this bizarre technique, or so they told us. It strengthened our coordination. A friend or two of mine might have said I needed the workout.

Over the next few weeks, I learned that basic training was not considered good enough for officer development. The physical exercise was brutal. But a curious thing began to happen. The young men in my outfit began to have a new respect for this "older woman." One day after a full-out sprint, a seventeen-year-old came over to me and said, "I want to shake your hand."

"Why's that?" I gasped, still trying to catch my breath.

"I was about to give up, but when I saw the determination on your face, I knew I had to keep going." Then he added what he really meant. "I couldn't let a girl beat me."

It was meant as a lovely compliment! From his point of view, I was acceptable. From then on, when I was called on to do cadence (which was quite often), one of the guys would yell, "Sir! Permission to relieve Strand." Of course, since I was twice their age, they took to calling me Gramma. At one point, fifty of them yelled for permission to relieve me (who says a soldier doesn't cry).

Then it dawned on me: that wily TAC officer knew exactly how to build team spirit. He taught those young men that women deserve their esteem, and he helped me earn a measure of respect.

If I hadn't figured it out for myself, it was confirmed one Sunday morning. I went to a nearby chapel where the congregation was African American. I loved the rock-and-roll and the dancing around the sanctuary. It all felt very free after weeks of toeing the line in training. One day the chaplain said to me, "Your TAC officer and I were talking when he saw you across the way. He said to me, 'That girl gives 110% to the program.'" Then the chaplain winked and smiled.

"Of course, if you ever tell him I told you, I'll deny it. But I thought you should know."

I wanted to hug him. But he was right; I kept it to myself and privately thrilled at the boost to my spirits.

SIDE-NOTE: Be Proud of Yourself

We've talked before about self-esteem. When you are good at something, it's okay to know it and show it. Oh, not as a boast or a sneer. You don't have to be a braggart, but you can surely demonstrate your abilities through your actions. You show your competence every time you add to a team or help someone else improve their performance. You persevered to become a rising star. Be confident that you're a person who others want around them. If you don't believe it, I challenge you to give it a try!

Graduation

Our six week of officer development saw us through a lot of training other than exercise. Olympians on the track and Einsteins in the classroom, at least that's how I thought of it.

Meanwhile, it seemed like everything we touched had to be in lockstep with each other. Fatigues pressed, starched, and hung evenly in our lockers. Boots spit-shined until you could see your face. Soap, toothbrush, toothpaste cap? You guessed it … spotless. One guy purchased a glycerin bar with a plastic wrap so it would look immaculate.

"What in tarnation is that?" the TAC sang out. "Looks like twenty-three demerits to me." So much for that guy's weekend.

Time passed. Finally, graduation was upon us. We were named the "Gold Flight" and stood at the front of the room while the others remained seated. We were called individually to shake hands with our Captain. Everyone was called except me. They skipped right over me, and I was terrorized by thoughts of failure. How was it possible? I'd given my all.

And then, the captain yelled, "Would Candidate Strand come to the front?"

Oh no! A public stoning? Hanging? I crept forward to the captain … and the classes began to applaud.

"Susan," he said. "What did you pay these guys?"

I couldn't even guess what he was talking about.

Then my TAC officer said, "Susan (the first time he called me by my given name), your classmates and I decided to award you the highest honor given to one who completes officer development. You are now my assistant for the next officer development class which starts tomorrow."

My mouth dropped. My classmates yelled, "GO GET'EM, STRAND!" And you know, I did just that. The next day, those newcomers didn't know what hit them.

"Okay, you mangy scumbags. I want those lockers spic and span by morning. No dirt in the corners. Lights out at twenty-one hundred and revelry at oh-four-hundred. We'll be taking a little stroll around base." I overheard my TAC officer whisper to a colleague, "I've created a monster. She was a nice girl when she came here."

CHAPTER TWO

Taking Flight

Helicopters have been called a lot of things, from devil birds to flying whales. But my first ride in a Hughes 300 was beautiful. She was a two-seater with bubble glass, the one that looked a little like a dragonfly. The first time up, my instructor whooshed us over a cliff. I gasped as the ground spilled away, and I grabbed the bottom of my seat.

Nothing had ever been so fantastic. It took my breath away. This is what I'd dreamed of for so long. Time and again, my learning disability, my gender, or my age had tried to derail me. But I persisted.

Back at the barracks, everyone chattered away about the experience. Some boasted about what a piece of cake it was. But I remained quiet, feeling reflective. I knew it wasn't going to be easy. I felt I had so much to prove. I was quietly thanking family, friends, and mostly the Lord for helping me find my way here.

In the days to come, we practiced, practiced, practiced. Some maneuvers came easily, others not so much. All of us had issues with hovering. We'd over-correct and swing like pendulums in the air. As the days passed, some began to do their solos. It was stressful to await my turn to fly alone, especially as more and more of the others were called on. Turns out it wasn't that I was a bad egg; my instructors and classmates were responsible for making me go last. The jerks planned it! Finally, I took off, circled the tower, then made my landing.

Phew!

But the ordeal wasn't over. It seems there was a tradition. The last to solo had to ride this silly bike (with a rotor on top) around all the other classes as they threw mugs of water. And I was it.

I was embarrassed, but off I rolled. It was clean watery fun, until one group dumped a garbage can of water on me. The wave hit me so hard, that it knocked me off the bike. I could quit, I suppose. But quitting was rarely an option in my book. So, I got back on the bike, and finished the route. Dismounting, I was disarrayed, shivering, and totally soaked. I looked for a hole to crawl into, but instead, I was met face to face by the base general.

"Candidate Strand," he said. "I congratulate you for finishing your ride. The class that emptied that barrel on you went entirely too far. They will be reprimanded." What a guy! Nobody ever dared say a word against him again, not in my presence. Back on the bike I returned down the road to a band of salutes.

Putting in Your Time

After you solo, you do a jillion flight miles, take offs, landings, and practice emergency procedures. And I did have an emergency. Once again, I found that the best way to control my fear was to follow the routines I had drilled into me.

I'd been called into the medical office for my penicillin tag before going out to the flight line. When I arrived on the field, my class had already left for the practice area. What a thrill being left all alone with MY helicopter. I did my walk around, checking the helicopter for any visible issues. I felt totally in control. I took off over the cliff, but immediately began to lose power. One of the first rules of flying in order to get enough airspeed is to point the nose of your aircraft downward. Every instinct shrieks to aim it up. My head took over from my fear, and I pulled her out of a stall.

We were all tested by check pilots to be sure we could pass muster with the Hughes 300. Next step would be other helicopters, often bigger or faster. We were all nervous, but fortunately, they didn't test for dry mouths or sweaty hands. Our scores went up on a blackboard when we finished for everyone to see. Following a pattern, I was last.

When the check pilot was about to write my score, I shut my eyes. I couldn't look. But then a cheer went up, and classmates were shaking my hand.

"You got an 85, Susan! Great score!"

And it was. Not perfect, but a very good score. I was moving on from the little bubble choppers I had come to love.

Hello Huey

The Huey is a large transport helicopter. The ships we began to fly had seen action in Vietnam. They were slow and loud, so maybe not great for combat situations, but they were reliable old girls.

One was gracious enough to put up with me while I tried to land when we practiced losing hydraulics. I just didn't have the upper body strength to control her. So I had more body work to do, and finally, I got the job done right.

After we passed the Huey class, we were ready for instrument flying. This is when you can't fly visually, which is usually due to weather.

I had not received an instrument rating in fixed-wing, and now I wished I had. It was a beast to conquer.

Two students rode in each chopper, taking turns doing maneuvers. One day, I felt spacey and didn't know which way was up. We landed, and I was sent to the flight surgeon's office. What was happening? Was I going into a coma again? I felt terrified.

A medic took my blood pressure and nearly panicked at how low it was. "I don't know how you got here. I'll go get the Flight Surgeon." The flight surgeon was too busy to see me, so I was to go back to the barracks and rest. Instead of waiting, a friend drove me to their family doctor. I was diagnosed with the flu and sent back to the barracks to wait it out.

I felt lousy by the time I got there, but not as lousy as I was about to feel. My Tac officer said the flight surgeon had taken me off flight status. "He's requested you not return to flying until a hearing can be conducted." The look of disbelief on his face no doubt mirrored the one on mine.

"But … but why? I just have the flu!"

He looked down. "I don't know. Now go rest."

While I waited for my hearing, I had my flight helmet adjusted. The major doing the job told me the truth. "The flight surgeon doesn't like having women in the Army. He'll see you're kicked out. But if you tell anyone what I said, I'll deny it."

I wasn't broken, but close to it. I would fight to be an airman. I'd speak my piece at the hearing. As it happened, I wasn't allowed to speak at all because I wasn't allowed to attend. Even the General couldn't help. "The flight surgeon is God in the Army. I'm so sorry. You're one of the best pilots we have. I know you won't let this stop you."

With more assurance than I felt, I said, "No. It won't."

And I began to plan my next move.

SIDE-NOTE: Facing Up to Roadblocks

No matter how much we might wish it to be different, sometimes there are mountains we can't climb. That's part of life. It's how we handle it that will matter in the long run.

Does it teach us empathy for others who face formidable odds? Make us more understanding of others? Are we wiser for the experience? Do we throw up our hands and give up? Heavens no! You've heard the phrase, "when the going gets tough, the tough get going." Perseverance and self-esteem have gotten you this far and will keep you moving ahead. You steel yourself with purpose to seek another approach. Your ability to do this is a measure of the success you have already achieved in your life.

CHAPTER THREE

What Next?

I couldn't fly with the Army, but that didn't mean I couldn't fly. I felt fortunate to have received the best training in the world, and now was the time to use it. And most of the men I met were not like that flight surgeon; he may have broken my heart, but not my spirit. I wouldn't let him humiliate me. I would prosper without him.

So, my disappointment wasn't debilitating. And I began to look in directions where, what I learned would be valued. I set my sights on commercial aviation.

To prepare, I needed my commercial license and instrument rating, which had been interrupted when I left the Army. Finding a helicopter wasn't easy. They weren't sitting around airports like the fixed-wing aircraft. And finding one I could afford to rent was another challenge. Finally, I found a small training helicopter in Long Beach, CA, called an R-22. It was about one tenth the size of a Huey. The day of my check ride was another challenge as the winds were over 20 knots. After about ten minutes up in the air my check pilot yelled, "Anyone who can fly this dixie-cup in these winds is a good pilot. You pass. Now get me down!"

I returned home to Phoenix, where I could revel in family times while I looked for work in a newspaper that advertised for pilots.

The whole "woman" issue raised its ugly head again.

"But you're a woman!" I heard from more potential employers than I care to remember.

This might have been worse in my day than in yours. We didn't have many laws that made it illegal to discriminate. Most men had never even thought about making way for their sisters! One thing about changing an attitude is that it takes time. And while there are still employers who hold women back, many have learned how they prosper by giving us a chance.

SIDE-NOTE Breaking Through

If your goal is a job that is traditionally not open to your race, gender, religion, or (whether it's legal or not), then realize it before you begin. The other candidates have a 100% chance ... your percent is substantially less. So do substantially more.

Know all there is to know about the employer before the interview. Demonstrate your interest not only in a job, but in their job. If your credentials are competitive enough to get you into the interview, then do you have other relevant skills that make you memorable? Maybe you know a foreign language, or you are a CNA or EMT. For a pilot who would have customers, my abilities with languages might be very welcome.

Be willing to take on a role in a smaller market before you reach for the top. A college teacher might start in a smaller school. A ballplayer starts in the minors. A pilot might fly shorter flights or smaller markets or lousy hours. Do it willingly.

Be sure to share more than the facts of your resume and the lessons you've learned along the way. In my case, I could demonstrate success through times of fear. My experience in Vietnam or in near misses on Pan Am? Very relevant to the employers I was trying to win over.

> *If you can't come up with a reason why you should win the job, then prepare to be passed over. Get your mindset right: you are worth it, and tell them why.*

Climbing the Ladder

The first man willing to give me a try owned a little Hughes bubble top, nearly identical to the dragonfly I learned to fly first. His job was to spray any growth on power lines. It wasn't glamorous – or even much fun – but I got my start.

My next boss had a charter service in Pennsylvania. He didn't seem to care that I was a woman and willingly gave me a chance. However, his chief co-pilot disagreed, so I had an enemy before I even met him.

The company owner eventually purchased a Sikorsky S-76 which was the first helicopter with wheels I ever flew. He checked me out in it, and by sheer luck (or maybe divine intervention), I made a perfect three-point landing. His co-pilot didn't fare as well, which the boss was tickled to tell him. "She was great! Outflew you, buddy."

After that, the co-pilot nearly hissed each time he saw me. We accepted each other as willingly as a cat and dog, both under order to get along. Nonetheless, the job was a good one, and I built up my flying time.

It ended soon after the boss had a tragic accident. He was pulling out of a field where he'd sprayed for gypsy moths, and he caught a skid of the Bell 206 on a powerline. The copter flipped and crashed upside down. While he lived, he was mentally and physically shattered. The business was soon lost, and I was looking for work once more.

I was ready, or at least I was cocky enough to think I was ready to work with the big shots. For a while, my resume flew from place to place, but I didn't. Finally, a company out of Louisiana flying to the oil rigs, expressed interest. They flew Aerospatiale Helicopters made in France and I immediately fell in love with them.

"Report at 8 am sharp," said one of the company men. "You'll be flying co-pilot out to one of the rigs." I met five of their pilots that evening, most with military experience. We talked flying experiences well into the evening. These guys cared a lot more about ability than gender. I felt surrounded by big brothers who wanted me to do well.

In the office the next morning, my colleague said, "You ready to spread your wings?"

"Sure am!" I answered although my knees were knocking.

"We'll be going about one hundred miles to the farthest offshore rig."

One hundred miles over open ocean? I thought. *Perfect! Sure, let's aim at the farthest one!* But I answered with a cheery, "Sounds great."

We walked to the helicopter, and my eyes lit up! She was another Aerospatiale but this time with two motors. It was love at first sight. "She's beautiful," I crooned over the silver and red chariot.

He knew I was nervous and proved to be a patient, understanding instructor. I wasn't experienced with this type of flying and learned fast that I had to depend on all that instrument instruction. With ocean everywhere and no defined horizon, you could get topsy-turvy in seconds.

"There it is," my co-worker announced.

"There what is?" I couldn't see a thing.

"Over there. That white speck."

My hands began to sweat. My mind swirled. How could you land on the head of a pin? Fortunately, my co-worker took over. "I don't want to scare you off on your first day. And the winds out here can dunk us in the drink pretty easily."

"Oh sure, no problem." *Thank Heaven!*

The rig was like a city in the sea. The guys might stare at me, but they were all gents. The pushiest thing ever said to me was "Sure nice to see a woman out here." The cafeteria food was scrumptious. After that first trip, the chef had a piece of chocolate cake ready for me whenever I landed. And there was a place for me to stay if the weather got too bad to make a return trip.

I loved this job. I was flying high, using the skills I'd learned. We'd fly to the rigs to pick up or deliver passengers or bring out a part. Winds of the Gulf went with the territory and hurricane speeds could whip up in a heartbeat. It could be scary, but I might have stayed in this job forever, but due to unforeseen circumstances, it was not meant to be. With nothing but respect for the men I had met and the confidence they'd helped me gain, I left for Phoenix once again.

I took another flight job or two after that, but the magic was over. I once even had to refuse a flight in poor weather, countermanding the boss's orders. The Army had taught me safety first, but I discovered that wasn't always true in commercial flying.

I realized flying the whirlybirds had been adventurous and fun, but I wasn't happy anymore. I thought it might be time to try something completely different.

Nobody told me I couldn't do just that.

PART VI
LOVE WHAT YOU DO

Susan Strand in a tandem parachute jump.

Chapter One

New Horizons

I wanted to see the world, and I did it.

I wanted to fly, and I did it.

The goals that I set for myself were under my belt, and I will always cherish both experiences. Loving what you do is an enormous achievement. We aren't put on this earth to be miserable, but it can happen if you don't keep your own wellbeing in mind.

Now I felt it was time to explore other trails. As you go through your life you develop curiosities that you might never have anticipated. I was ready to apply skills I'd learned to occupations I had never tried but sounded intriguing.

I gave it a lot of thought. What did I really need in a job to make me happy?

- **I like a challenge.** How many times had I proved this to myself? Riding that too big bike as a pre-schooler. Overcoming shyness to try out for the Junior Miss Pageant. Working the Vietnam flights for Pan-Am. Flying to distant specks in the ocean time and again. Working successfully in jobs usually reserved for the boys. It is in my DNA to be challenged. I needed a job that could do that.

- **I like animals.** There was Tico, my chihuahua, when I was a kid. And so many horses available to ride. However, being on the move so much in my life, I had not been able to keep a companion animal. Maybe a job involving animals would be fun. Spending summers on my grandparents' farm when I was a child had prepared me to love the outdoors. Animals and outdoors. Yes, that sounded great.

- **I like sharing my experiences with others.** Half the joy of doing so much and seeing so many places was to share it with others. Maybe I'd find a place where people wanted to hear what I had to say.

- **I like to travel.** That passion to pack up and go has never left me. I'd love a job that still allowed me to move around the country.

National Transportation Safety Board

My first foray into something-completely-different was a huge disaster. I hated it almost as much as that frat party back in college. Hey, we all make mistakes sometimes.

I was to be the first female air safety investigator for NTSB (National Transportation

Safety Board). I'd worked for cops, and I was a pilot; who could have better credentials? But the all-male staff clearly didn't want me there. I'd worked through that issue before, but not this time. I was harassed daily until I filed a report with the Federal Discrimination Board, but even that didn't stop it. These were not the types of animals I had in mind!

Frankly, I quickly found I didn't want the job anyway. Investigating accidents was miserable; I once pulled human flesh from an instrument panel. The Discrimination Board eventually ruled in my favor. It didn't soothe all the anger I felt, but it helped. I was given a year's pay as long as I left the NTSB. I can't say this was exactly a tragedy for anyone.

Park Ranger

Hey, I thought. *Why not?* It suited my enjoyment of animals, nature, and the great outdoors. Helping travelers love our public lands felt like work that mattered. This could be perfect.

There was just one problem: everyone wanted to be a park ranger! There were no permanent jobs to be had. Okay, at least there were seasonal positions, but they had no health insurance and paid minimum wage. Who wouldn't want a bargain like that?

But I recalled the lessons of the steppingstones. I would get my toe in the door starting with seasonal positions ... permanent placement would surely come. I'd keep applying every chance I got at national facilities around the country.

My first seasonal placement was at the Grand Canyon. Three of us were to room in an old trailer that was a dump on the outside and even worse on the inside. I was forty, and my roomies were in college, so I knew I was also to be a housemother. Only walks in the beautiful park kept me sane.

I quickly learned I was far more interested in doing interpretive talks than in taking tolls, so the Canyon job wasn't for me. I next took a position as an interpretive ranger on the Blue Ridge Parkway in Virginia. I loved being on stage in front of an audience. My mom always said I was a ham. After my talks, the audience and I ventured outside to find wildlife. If it was dark, we covered flashlights in red cellophane so animals wouldn't see us. I felt at one with nature.

The next seasonal stop was at the visitor center on the USS Arizona Memorial in Honolulu. Nine hundred men were entombed inside that memorial. I did my best to always honor the horror of the day in a way my audience could feel it, too. It is an unforgettable experience to be there.

The Florida Everglades awaited me next. It was (and is) an area under stress from land development and water drainage. I became a harbinger for the problems it faced; the Discovery Channel even gave me screentime in their documentary on the situation. Imagine me, on national television! It certainly gave me my fifteen-minutes of fame within the park service. The birds were amazing in the swamps and grasslands. But I admit I met other animals that weren't quite so likable. While encroachment threatened all of the Everglades, my own personal threat was mosquitos. Mercy! Every morning I put my uniform over a chair on my patio and sprayed it with insect repellent. Then I doused myself in lotion, rushed outside to jump on my bike and ride like the wind to work. Sometimes I beat the mosquitos to the door!

But the really shocking animal encounters were with the alligators. They were often in the parking lot of the Royal Palm Visitor Center, lumbering from one water hole to another. I was to position myself between the animal and visitors, not allowing the one to get too close to the other. Keep in mind, the gators had not read the same employee manual.

One day I was saying, "Not too close … they can move really fast." Meanwhile, one tippy toed up behind me. I heard a hiss. I turned in slow motion to see a huge mouth baring its lovely sharp teeth. Visitors that day observed the miracle of a ranger flying through the air. That gator may still be telling its offspring the story!

After a year in the Everglades, I moved west again to Montezuma Castle in Arizona. It is an ancient Native American ruin high on a canyon wall. I was in great awe of its structure, built centuries ago of mud and sticks. I discovered the strength of that mud for myself hiking one day in a fresh batch of caliche … the local name for it is nature's cement. It was so heavy, I could hardly lift my legs.

I loved my co-workers, Kath, Babs, and Sarah. John—my other friend at the post—and I competed daily with how many dollar bills we could take in from tourists. This was as congenial a group of co-workers as I ever had, a fine memory of smiles and laughter.

Then, for something completely different, I moved to Fort Clatsop National Monument in Astoria, Oregon. My parents (and their little dog) joined me for a summer in a manufactured home we rented. Fort Clatsop was the farthest point of the Lewis and Clark expedition. It was a delight to work there. We wore period costumes inside the fort replica, telling tales of bygone days. We fired an ancient rifle for the crowd, made candles, spun wool, and walked trails, pointing out plants used for medication and food. Some of the rangers even demonstrated digging out a canoe.

Reliving history helped bring it alive for visitors and for us. I remember it as one of my most joyful summers at work in the fort and relaxing at the "homestead" with my folks.

All this time, I was working as a seasonal worker. After 700 rejected applications, a superintendent finally found me a permanent job with the park service. Did I mention *perseverance*? If you're like me, you'll never take no for an answer, no matter how long it takes to get a yes!

Permanent Employment at Last

I began my permanent assignment at Casa Grande Ruins National Monument in Coolidge, Arizona. The caliche (mud and stick) house I lived in had been built in the 1930s with walls thick enough to temper the heat or cold, depending on the season. And I finally had companion animals! Great Horned Owls swooped down for drinks of water. An enormous toad leaped out of one of the water bowls one evening went I went to fill it. We scared each other darn near out of our skins! Cottontails, jackrabbits, quail, and coyotes stopped by to pay their respects.

At work, the old building stayed so cool, I wore long johns year-round. In the summer, I'd quickly change out of them if I went outdoors where it might be 124 degrees. One day—while I was watching a visitor's kids put their sticky figures on the glass door I had just cleaned—I looked up to see the man who had been my teacher in the seventh grade. All these years later, I remembered him, and even more surprising, he remembered me. He and his wife asked me to their home for dinner.

He told her he had me conduct classes from time to time.

"Why?" She asked.

"Because Susan was the smartest."

If I hadn't already admired that man, I would have started then and there. Obviously, he had superior taste!

The worker bees at Casa Grande had diversity down pat long before the word became popular. We were Native American, Hispanic, and in my case, mostly Scandinavian.

Unfortunately, sexism raised its head here as it had so often before. The male rangers with permanent positions pushed most of the work onto me and the rest of the staff. I discovered I didn't receive recommendations to transfer because the superintendent wanted to keep his "beast of burden" in place. My time there is not a good memory for me.

I marked time until retirement, which wasn't far away. Meanwhile, I learned more about the rangers I worked with. As I mentioned earlier in this story, I was dumbfounded by how miserable some people's childhoods had been. Here in Casa Grande, I heard the tales of stepparent beatings … alcoholic parents … child abandonment. Here more than anywhere else, I found how bitter life could be for people with miserable upbringings. They made life more difficult for the people around them, as well as for themselves. These were people forced to live with "I wish I had" instead of climbing toward the best that life could be. It's a deep hole to dig out of, but I hope for each and every reader, you can make that climb.

CHAPTER TWO

Next Stop, Alaska

I had been curious about Glacier Bay National Park. I'd heard rangers board cruise ships while in the bay. How fun that sounded! Yep, Susan took aim at a new goal.

Before retirement from my permanent role with the park service, I applied once again for a seasonal position in Glacier Bay. It would be a great experience for my resume if I wanted one of those cruise jobs. As a ranger, I gave talks on the ships and commentary from the bridge. Once in a while, we led hikes through the forest.

Once I had a dozen people with me when one man yelled, "Susan, don't move! There is a large black bear in the tree just above you."

Help, I thought. Where's a ranger when you need one? Oh, that's me!

I ordered everyone to move slowly backward. Treat the bear with respect; speak only in a soothing manner. One terrified woman shrieked, "HI THERE, BEAR. WHAT A GOOD-LOOKING FELLOW." It scared that bear so badly that he flew out of that tree on the run in the opposite direction, while I fought the urge to gallop off in the other. I knew how close to disaster we came, but my dozen hikers didn't. They loved it! "Thank you, Susan, for providing us with a black bear. What a tale to tell when we get back home. When do we get to see a grizzly?" They thought I was great; I thought they were nuts!

After having been "chased" in my life by a bull, an alligator, and now a bear, I thought I might be done with animal antics. But no. In the dark, walking to work, I interrupted a moose with her calf. They were crossing the road when I startled them. Do you have any idea how big and aggressive a mama moose can be? I hoped not to find out, so I switched on my flashlight and swung it side to side as fast as I could. That mama looked at me and must have thought I was as crazy as those bear tourists. She bolted in her direction as I bolted in mine, an employee very eager to get to work.

The summer ended, and that year, my parents and I moved to Washington State. Once settled, I applied to the cruise lines going to

Alaska to be the naturalist working on ships, giving lectures in the theatre and commentaries from the bridge. Celebrity Cruises agreed that my experience as a ranger was an asset; I soon had a job.

My first time on the bridge addressing the ship, I announced, "Welcome to Alaska!" A very stern Greek captain scowled at me. Moments later, I had to clarify, "I mean, we're in British Columbia, but we'll soon welcome you to Alaska!"

Since things couldn't get worse, they got better. A passenger was sick, so a Coast Guard helicopter was coming to pick him up. I told the captain I was a pilot if he needed help in any way.

He, and the rest of the male officers on the bridge, looked amazed. "Yes, please, Susan. Would you stay on the bridge and communicate with the pilot? My English is not the best. You can relay my instructions."

The helicopter couldn't land due to furious winds and rain, so it removed the patient in a basket as it hovered above. All went well. And that's how my experience as a helicopter pilot saved my job as a naturalist. Never say you can't!

I was well into my second season as a cruise naturalist when I contracted a severe bronchial infection. I fought it with antibiotics for four seasons but finally had to leave for good. My bronchial tubes were shot. I returned home to Washington, where I live to this day.

CHAPTER THREE

Life can throw us many curve balls. I have lost both my parents, and my own life is limited, or so the doctors say. I could feel sorry for myself—and sometimes I do—but I chose to take a different route. I listened to the advice of the people around me.

"You should write a book," some said.

"Oh, phooey. Who's gonna read some stranger's story?" I thought it silly and egotistical.

"But it would be such an inspiration to others." Well, okay. Maybe. If the world travels and private miracles of a retiree can inspire others to climb mountains they thought impossible, well, okay. Maybe.

What finally did it was a woman in a rehabilitation center who asked me to come tell my story. I didn't want to speak; I wasn't a recovering addict or parolee. I never overcame the issues they faced.

"That's the point," said the woman. "I want them to see what life can be like when you rise above obstacles. I promise it will be worth it."

And it was. They listened with rapt attention as I talked about my journey: "braindead" to glory days at Pan Am, to helicopter pilot, to the National Park Service. They empathized with the sexism and endless bureaucracy along the way. They wanted to hear what I had to say. They wanted to believe that they, too, had the God-given potential to pull themselves up from the darkest moments to attain some of their most cherished dreams. They gathered enough strength to tell me their stories.

And so, I wrote this book, my little dog Angel at my side. I hope it helps young and old alike find a better motto than "I wish I had." We each have a daring explorer hidden inside, waiting to break free. Let go and live your life. If you try, you are never a failure, and you will have no regrets.

"I skydived a while back, now I think I will try zip lining."

Susan's Steps for Success

- *Measure success in the trying.*
- *Don't tie yourself down.*
- *Persevere.*
- *Be proud of yourself.*
- *Don't listen to naysayers.*
- *Learn to face down fears.*
- *Make a plan but stay flexible.*
- *Roadblocks happen; be patient.*
- *Allow yourself to be happy.*
- *Have faith.*

ACKNOWLEDGEMENTS

Without doubt support from the Lord and my wonderful parents.

Ms. Katherine Suter for all her wisdom and encouragement.

Colonel Richard Glasebrook, USAF, Ret. for all his help without which I would never have gotten into flight school and become a helicopter pilot.

All the doctors, esp. Dr. Robert Briggs, and nurses at the Barrows Neurological Institute in Phoenix, AZ for their constant diligence during my three months in a coma.

Dr. Wm. O. Smith and his wife Ann for all their guidance and prayers through my early years.

Carolyn Grisz Harrison without whose help I would never have become a Pan American World Airways Stewardess allowing me to see the world and meet so many people from all walks of life—even a U.S. President and the king and queen of Denmark.

Katie Phillips who has helped me so much with finances after my retirement.

Addie Weiland for all her prayers and being God's Angel.

This book would not have been possible without the help of Linda B. Myers and Heidi Hansen.

And a special thank you to all those along my path of life who have been there with a helping hand.

To all those listed "May the Lord bless and keep you and make His face to shine upon you."

ABOUT THE AUTHOR

Susan M. Strand grew up in Arizona. After graduating from Arizona State University, she became a stewardess with Pan American World Airways. Ten years later she would become one of the first women trained by the military in helicopters. The following decade, she worked for the NTSB as the first woman air safety investigator. Finding the job depressing, she decided to try Park Ranger with the National Park Service. When she retired fifteen years later to the Pacific Northwest, she worked as a Naturalist on cruise ships going to Alaska for five years. Her last job took her to West Virginia as a house mother of a sorority.

Susan's next endeavor is to go on a speaking tour to not only promote this book but to encourage people of all walks of life to follow their dreams and never say "I wish I had."

Desiderata

Go placidly amid the noise and the haste, and remember what peace there may be in silence. As far as possible, without surrender, be on good terms with all persons. * **Speak your truth** quietly and clearly; and listen to others, even to the dull and the ignorant; they too have their story.   *   **Avoid loud** and aggressive persons; they are vexatious to the spirit. If you compare yourself with others, you may become vain or bitter, for always there will be greater and lesser persons than yourself.   *   **Enjoy your achievements** as well as your plans. Keep interested in your own career, however humble; it is a real possession in the changing fortunes of time. *

Exercise caution in your business affairs, for the world is full of trickery. But let this not blind you to what virtue there is; many persons strive for high ideals, and everywhere life is full of heroism. * **Be yourself.** Especially do not feign affection. Neither be cynical about love; for in the face of all aridity and disenchantment, it is as perennial as the grass. * **Take kindly** the counsel of the years, gracefully surrendering the things of youth. * **Nurture strength** of spirit to shield you in sudden misfortune. But do not distress yourself with dark imaginings. Many fears are born of fatigue and loneliness.   *   Beyond a wholesome discipline, **be gentle** with yourself. You are a child of the universe no less than the trees and the stars; you have a right to be here. And whether or not it is clear to you, no doubt the universe is unfolding as it should. Therefore be at peace with God, whatever you conceive Him to be. And whatever your labors and aspirations, in the noisy confusion of life, keep peace in your soul. With all its sham, drudgery and broken dreams, it is still a beautiful world. Be cheerful. **Strive to be happy.**